Living on the Edge
WHITEWATER RAFTING

Shane McFee

PowerKiDS press.

New York

Published in 2008 by The Rosen Publishing Group, Inc.
29 East 21st Street, New York, NY 10010

First Edition

Editor: Joanne Randolph
Book Design: Kate Laczynski
Photo Researcher: Jessica Gerweck

Photo Credits: CVR, p. 1 © www.istockphoto.com/Phily Berry; p. 4 © www.istockphoto.com/Özgür Donmaz; p. p. 6 © John Beatty/Getty Images, Inc.; p. 8 © www.istockphoto.com/Daniel Stein; p. 10 © www.istockphoto.com/Leah-Anne Thompson; p. 12 © www.istockphoto.com/Nancy DenBak; p. 14 © www.istockphoto.com/Loic Bernard; p. 16 © www.istockphoto.com; p. 18 © www.istockphoto.com/Dylan Jones; p. 20 Shutterstock.com.

Library of Congress Cataloging-in-Publication Data

McFee, Shane.
   Whitewater rafting / Shane McFee. — 1st ed.
      p. cm. — (Living on the edge)
   Includes index.
   ISBN 978-1-4042-4218-0 (library binding)
   1. Rafting (Sports)—Juvenile literature. I. Title.
   GV780.M34 2008
   797.12'1—dc22
                                        2007034537

Manufactured in the United States of America

CONTENTS

4

Riding the Rapids

Sometimes water in a river flows so quickly it looks white. These fast-moving parts of rivers are called whitewater rapids. This water is very powerful.

People enjoy riding whitewater rapids in small boats called rafts. Thousands of people go whitewater rafting every year.

Whitewater rafting can be **dangerous** because the water is fast and powerful. Rafts do not have engines. Whitewater rafters fight the rapids and direct the rafts with paddles. Most rafters enjoy the danger. It is a **thrill**. Do you want to learn more about this **extreme sport**? Keep reading!

Do not go whitewater rafting if you do not want to get wet! This sport is enjoyed by thousands of people every year.

All About Rafting

Rafting is one of the oldest forms of **transportation** in the world. People have used rafts for thousands of years. A raft is a flat object that floats. People tied wood together to make the first rafts. People used rafts to float food, animals, and building supplies down rivers.

Rafting did not become a sport done for fun until the 1960s. **Commercial** rafting companies offered trips on the Colorado River through the Grand Canyon. The sport spread to other places with whitewater rapids.

There are commercial rafting companies all over the world. Here a group of people takes a whitewater rafting tour of the Grand Canyon in Arizona.

What Is Whitewater?

Water is one of the most powerful forces on Earth. Whitewater rapids are some of the strongest forms of water.

Rapids can be created in different ways. A river's slope can create rapids. Every river has a slope. A slope is a hill. When the slope is steep, the river flows quickly. Waterfalls have very steep slopes.

Sometimes rivers become narrow. Other times they become filled with a lot of rain or melting snow. In both cases, this means that more water is pushed through a smaller space. This can cause rapids to form.

These are the rapids at Great Falls on the Potomac River, near Washington, D.C. The river breaks into two narrow parts, which causes the rapids to form.

What You Need

The most important thing you need for whitewater rafting is a raft. Most rafts today are made of a special kind of rubber. They are filled with air. This allows them to float.

You also need paddles to go whitewater rafting. Whitewater paddles may look like any other boat paddles, but they are made for rapids. Another important supply for whitewater rafting is the **life jacket**. It helps you float in case you fall out of the raft. Whitewater rafters should always wear life jackets. Rapids will force even the best swimmers under water.

Many rafters wear helmets. A helmet keeps a rafter's head from getting hurt if he or she hits rocks and fallen trees under the water.

In a Class by Itself

Most rafts hold more than one person. This means several different rafters are paddling at the same time. They have to work together in order to get through the rapids safely.

There are six classes of rapids. Class 1 rapids are safe and easy to get through. Beginners should raft in class 1 rapids. Class 2 rapids are a little riskier. Class 5 rapids are very hard to raft through. Only master rafters should try them. Class 6 rapids can be deadly. Sometimes they even have waterfalls.

This is an overhead look at part of the Whirlpool Rapids and the whirlpool at Niagara Falls. The Whirlpool Rapids are class 6 rapids.

Not Just for Rafts

Not everyone who rides rapids is a rafter. Some people use special boats called canoes and kayaks. Canoes are like rowboats. Whitewater canoes are made for moving through rapids.

Kayaks look like long, skinny canoes. Most kayaks are built for one person. The kayak pilot uses a special paddle. Kayak paddles are long and have blades on both ends. Kayaks are easier to direct than canoes and rafts. Kayaks are not as **stable** as rafts, though. This means that kayaks are more likely to tip over in rapids. A good kayaker can flip the kayak right side up.

This woman is doing a sport called freestyle kayaking. In this sport, she stays in one spot on the rapids and does special tricks or moves.

In It to Win

Most whitewater rafters ride the rapids for fun. Some whitewater rafters are good enough to **compete**. They have races to see which teams can travel the fastest through hard rapids. People from all over the world compete at whitewater rafting. Whitewater rafting has even been a sport in the Summer Olympics.

Whitewater canoeing and kayaking will be events in the 2008 Summer Olympics. The paddlers will paddle through very fast and bumpy rapids. They will also have to direct their boats through special gates.

These people are competing in a whitewater rafting contest in Russia. Their raft is specially built to let them move quickly through the rapids.

Rafting on the Job

Not every rafter rides whitewater for fun. Some rafters do it to earn a paycheck.

Some of these rafters are guides. Guides are master rafters. Many rafting companies hire guides to lead trips through rapids. Guides are good teachers. They have a short amount of time to teach beginning rafters how to paddle. They are **responsible** for leading beginning rafters through the rapids safely.

Some rafters are rescue workers. This means they save people who are in trouble. They are called swiftwater rescuers. Swiftwater rescuers train to be excellent rafters. Swiftwater rescuers look for missing rafters and boaters.

You can see the guide wearing the black helmet in this photo. Guides make sure that beginners who want to ride the rapids stay safe.

Staying Safe

Danger is always part of whitewater rafting, but **injuries** are few. Most rafters are very careful. Most guides are very good at what they do. Commercial rafting companies will not allow people to raft if the weather has made the rapids too rough.

Whitewater rafting is safer today than it was years ago. Guides have more training. Rafts and kayaks are better and safer.

Remember, thousands of people enjoy rafting every year without injuries. This does not mean that whitewater rafting is a safe sport, though. The danger is what makes it fun.

Part of staying safe on rapids is choosing rapids that match up with your skills. There are many easy rapids where families can safely enjoy this sport.

Living on the Edge

Whitewater rafting is one of the only ways to **explore** some of the world's most beautiful rivers. Does it sound like fun? Do you want to learn how to ride the rapids? Ask your mother and father to help you find a commercial rafting center. These centers teach you how to ride rapids safely.

Do you have rapids near you? In the United States, many people enjoy whitewater rafting in Arizona, California, Colorado, Maine, North Carolina, Oregon, Washington, West Virginia, and many other places with powerful rivers. Maybe whitewater rafting is the sport for you.

GLOSSARY

commercial (kuh-MER-shul) Having to do with business or trade.

compete (kum-PEET) To go against another in a game or test.

dangerous (DAYN-jeh-rus) Might cause hurt.

explore (ek-SPLOR) To travel over little-known land.

extreme sport (ek-STREEM SPORT) A bold and uncommon sport, such as street luge, skateboarding, BMX, and wakeboarding.

injuries (INJ-reez) Hurts done to a person's body.

life jacket (LYF JA-ket) A special piece of clothing that makes a body float in the water.

responsible (rih-SPON-sih-bul) Having the duty of taking care of someone or something.

stable (STAY-bul) Not easily moved or tipped.

thrill (THRIL) A feeling of pleasure.

transportation (tranz-per-TAY-shun) A way of traveling from one place to another.

INDEX

WEB SITES

Due to the changing nature of Internet links, PowerKids Press has developed an online list of Web sites related to the subject of this book. This site is updated regularly. Please use this link to access the list:
www.powerkidslinks.com/edge/raft/